LOOK! A FLUTTERBY!

Bil Keane

To Mom —
Merry Christmas
1995
Love, Jim + Lois

FAWCETT GOLD MEDAL • NEW YORK

A Fawcett Gold Medal Book
Published by Ballantine Books
Copyright © 1992 by Bil Keane
Distributed by King Features Syndicate, Inc.

Library of Congress Catalog Card Number: 92-97256

ISBN 0-449-14810-6

Manufactured in the United States of America

First Edition: April 1993

"Aren't you glad I got into the
family, Mommy? You don't have
to be the only girl."

"Mine's closest! I win!"

"Why this poor mark in 'Listening
Comprehension'?...Billy? Why
this poor mark in..."

"Grandma sent a postcard from
New Hamster."

"Could you sew our ball right away,
Mommy? The bases are loaded!"

"We picked it out and Mommy paid
for it with a little card."

"We each get 22 keys."

"That's printing and this is cursive
writing. In cursive all the
letters hold hands."

"The kitchen has a better
dance floor."

"Your tea looks like you forgot
to remove the price tag."

"Epistles are the Apostles' wives."

"Is that manny-kin wearin' a wig,
or is it her own hair?"

"Well, I'm off to
the rat race."

"Kittycat wants
to go, too!"

"'Stead of bein' allergic to
chocolate, couldn't I be
allergic to squash?"

"I love you, Mommy, you're so...so
high in fiber, low in sodium,
so cholesterol free..."

"Those are the air holes for
the blackbirds."

"Who shot the pencil at you?"

"Jeffy, I sincerely hope nobody ever
hires you as a tanker captain."

"Why does everybody hafta say
'OOOOH' and 'AHHHH'?"

"I don't like 'Jack and Jill' or
'Humpty Dumpty.' They fell and
broke things."

"But I didn't turn up my nose,
Mommy. God did it."

"It's an educational toy, PJ. If
Daddy trips over it, you'll
learn plenty."

"Water's a bit hot, Jeffy.
Can you stand it?"
"I can stand it, but I can't
sit it."

"PJ escaped into the next cell!"

"Did these used to be REAL animals?"

"One of the good things about cones
is you can eat the package."

"How do they get the seeds out
of these grapes without
makin' holes?"

"You're a terrible cook, Dolly.
This is the worst mud
I've ever eaten."

"...and say hi to St. Maria Goretti
'cause we go to her church."

"How come they're always asleep when
we pass something interesting?"

"How far back was that gas
station we stopped at?"

"Find out if they have a soda machine, Daddy, and a sliding board in the pool, and cable TV, and candies on the pillow..."

"The toilet seat must be broken.
They tied it together with
a paper ribbon."

"Not for me. I like to
eat kneeling."

"Look, Mommy! A piece of salad!"

"Mommy! Jeffy's tracking sand
into the ocean!"

"Who put soap in the ocean?"

"Maybe we'll catch a
loudmouth bass!"

"Mmm! The ocean's trimmin' the
beach with whipped cream!"

"I don't like swimmin' in the
ocean 'cause it won't
stand still."

"I've got sand in my shoes!"

"I think this p-pony needs
n-new sh-shocks."

"I'm tryin' to wash the sand
off my lollipop."

"Why do the waves keep
foldin' over?"

"Can we take some sand home with us
and grow our own beach?"

"Cows never run 'cause they don't
want their milk to get fizzy."

"Mommy! I'm really growin' up!
I hiccupped!"

"Grandma! Did you tell PJ he could
read your magazine?"

"Don't touch, Jeffy! It might
be poison ivory."

"Okay, Dr. Hareski, he's yours till
Thursday. Check him over, give
him his shots..."

"I'm glad you aren't fat, Daddy.
I was the first one finished
beading belts."

"Mommy, could we run the vacuum
cleaner to clean somethin' up?"

"Bless Mommy and the whole works."

"When you were little, Grandma,
were you the only one in your
class with gray hair?"

"Mommy, next time I want to go to
the haunted house, don't
let me go."

"The three games PJ likes best
are peekaboo, patty-cake
and tickle."

"Does Mommy know you're playing
with her toys?"

"I'm always 'too little to do
things' and 'big enough
to know better.'"

"Louder, Mommy!"

"No salad dressing, Mommy! Just
leave my lettuce blank."

"You said it'd be tomorrow when I
got up, and it's TODAY."

"I don't see any of those
air lions."

"Are there any hugs left in your
arms for me?"

"High-ho the stereo, the farmer
in the well..."

"Mommy's cleaning out the attic."

"Grandma, can we switch to a
station that gets THESE days
instead of THOSE days?"

"Mommy! She wants to know if I'll
hold. Hold what?"

"Could we buy another set of
blocks, Mommy? I need
another 'F'."

"Do the tacks hold the
ham together?"

"You'll hafta take over all the
petting and ear-scratching,
Mommy."

"I can't wait till I'm in the eighth grade and know all there is to know."

"I tried the white crayon but
it doesn't work."

"Listen, Mommy! This is our
phone number."

"Wait, Daddy!"   "Okay, you can
drill now."

"The crowd really likes Daddy's
line calls. Whenever he yells
"OUT" they all whistle."

"Maybe Barfy found the
Keebler elves."

"We tried out a new teacher today."

"I feel sorry for that horse. He
has no place to go."

"Look, Daddy! Homemade flowers!"

"If I grow up and get Willard Scott's job, I'm gonna order sunshine every day."

"Here he comes — the leader of disorganized grime."

"That's a good story. Can we get
the video?"

"Why can't WE be in the picture
with you?"

"They're marshmallows, Jeffy —
not Nerf candy."

"Wave harder, PJ. How do you
'spect Daddy to see that little
MICROWAVE of yours?"

"My favorite Italian food
— little pillows!"

"I can't order, Mommy. There
aren't any pictures on
the menu."

"I think the Kesslers' cat is broken.
They're takin' him to the vet's
to have him fixed."

"Who trained them to do that?"

"Well, I guess it's up and
let 'em at me."

"Those sticks are helpin' that tree
grow 'cause they remember when
THEY were a little tree."

"Can you microwave my lunch, Mommy?
The guys are waiting."

"Why didn't her mother tell her
not to talk to wolves?"

"Mommy, can you open up the
sky for me?"

"Somehow I feel like a zookeeper."

"We're starting a newspaper. You can be in it if you do something exciting."

"You can't have the TWO best jobs
on the paper, Billy! Which one
do y'want — Editor
or Cartoonist?"

"I get the most 'portant job —
Cartoonist. YOU can be Editor."

"We don't want Daddy on our paper.
He worked for the Philadelphia
Bulletin and it folded."

"Does anybody wanna buy an ad
in the Family Times for
a dollar?"

"Do my homework? Mommy! What about
'freedom of the press'?"

"I'm coverin' sports for The Family
Times, Daddy. How many golf balls
did you lose yesterday?"

"Time to put the paper to bed."

"Any ideas how we might get our
paper printed, Daddy? AND NO
FAIR READIN' IT!"

"How much longer will the copier
be tied up with the press run
of this 'Family Times'?"

"Paper, lady? We'll READ it
to you!"

"Putting a newspaper together is
fun. The hard part is
DELIVERIN' IT!"

"I keep sneezin', Mommy. Maybe
I'm 'lergic to somethin'
around here."

"I KNOW who did it, but
I'll ask anyway."

"Will you unwrap this for me?"

"I'll bet it's very hard to learn
to draw Chinese."

"If you want to be a waitress when you grow up, Dolly, you hafta learn to say, 'There you go.' "

"Wait, PJ! The
water's hot."

"If you're lookin' for Daddy,
he's over helping Mr. Spero
watch the game."

"PJ, I love you from the bottom of
my heart. Mommy and Daddy
are in the top part."

"But everybody laughs when Lucy
does it to Charlie Brown."

"Where's the lid to my sandwich?"

"You've got another pound to love, Mommy!"

"Mommy, will you come look for my
blue sweatshirt? You're a better
finder than Daddy."

"When you finish shaving you hafta
put little bloody pieces of
paper on your face."

"Mommy! I tried to turn on the lamp
and it took a picture!"

"Well, you just wait till I grow up
and I'm your BIG sister!"